THE ZEN OF OZ

Ten Spiritual Lessons from Over the Rainbow

JOEY GREEN

ILLUSTRATIONS BY CATHY PAVIA

CALLIGRAPHY BY SUMI NISHIKAWA

RENAISSANCE BOOKS
Los Angeles

Library of Congress Cataloging-in-Publication Data

Green, Joey.
        The zen of Oz / Joey Green.
                p. cm.
        ISBN 1-58063-020-0 (alk. paper)
        1. Baum, L. Frank (Lyman Frank), 1856–1919. Wizard of Oz.
        2. Children's stories, American—History and criticism.
        3. Fantastic fiction, American—History and criticism.
        4. Baum, L. Frank (Lyman Frank), 1856–1919—Religion.
        5. Spiritual life—Zen Buddhism. 6. Oz (Imaginary place)
        I. Title.
        PS3503.A923W598 1998
        813'.4—dc21   98-36394
                                                             CIP

10 9 8 7 6 5 4 3 2 1

Design by Lisa-Theresa Lenthall

Distributed by St. Martin's Press
Manufactured in the United States of America
First Edition

To the Young at Heart

CONTENTS

THE ZEN OF OZ

Somewhere,
Over the rainbow,
Skies are blue,
And the dreams
That you dare to dream
Really do come true.
　　　　—E. Y. Harburg and Harold Arlen

INTRODUCTION

The Wizard of Oz has probably been seen more times by more people than any other film in motion picture history. Every time this classic American film is broadcast on television, millions of people tune in to watch Dorothy, the Scarecrow, the Tin Man, and the Cowardly Lion journey down the Yellow Brick Road. Why do so many people love *The Wizard of Oz* so dearly? What is it about this movie that captures our hearts? Why are we so eager to watch it time and time again?

Everyone knows that *The Wizard of Oz* is rich with meaning. The movie has an inspiring homespun philosophy all its own. As the movie's opening dedication succinctly states, "Time has been powerless to put its kindly philosophy out of fashion."

But what exactly is *The Wizard of Oz*'s "kindly philosophy"?

Dorothy tries to sum it all up before leaving Oz. "It's that if ever I go looking for my heart's desire again, I won't look any further than my own backyard," she tells Glinda, the Good Witch of the North. "Because if it isn't there, I never really lost it to begin with. Is that it?"

"That's all it is," confirms Glinda.

But is that really all there is to *The Wizard of Oz*? Or is there something much deeper going on? Does *The Wizard of Oz* touch a spiritual chord in each one of us because it has a certain Zen to it?

When Dorothy spirals back to Kansas and wakes up in her bed, she learns that she was bumped on the head and knocked unconscious during the cyclone. Her trip to Oz, Aunt Em insists, was simply a bad dream.

"No, but it wasn't a dream," protests Dorothy. "It was a place!"

Toto, the only one who could possibly confirm Dorothy's story, remains speechless. Dorothy never looks under her blanket to see if the ruby slippers are still on her feet. Would Dorothy simply insist that the ruby slippers fell off during her dizzying flight back home (possibly killing yet another wicked witch)? Or is Dorothy, limited by her adolescent vocabulary, trying to tell us something much more profound? Could she be trying to convey the idea that Oz is a state of mind—a kind of enlightenment like *nirvana*? And isn't it odd that the word Oz resembles the word *om*, the universal sound used as a mantra to reach a transcendental state of mind from which to contemplate the ultimate reality?

When Dorothy exclaims, "Oh, Auntie Em, there's no place like home," she is actually, on a deeper level, sharing a key Zen principle: You already possess the attributes you seek most passionately.

Upon closer examination, I discovered that the entire movie overflows with Zen wisdom.

Oz is actually governed by the Tao, the totally spontaneous creative force in the universe that can do everything by doing nothing.

Glinda, the Good Witch of the North, is clearly a Zen Master. She sets Dorothy on the Yellow Brick Road to spiritual enlightenment. When Dorothy, the Scarecrow, the Tin Man, and the Cowardly Lion let go of their conscious yearning and free their minds to function spontaneously and in harmony with the cosmos, brains, heart, and courage flow easily and effortlessly. Ultimately, Dorothy attains *satori*, the Zen experience of "awakening." She finds her true Self, her higher consciousness, her ultimate Oneness with the cosmos, her home.

You already easily understand and embrace the beautiful messages in *The Wizard of Oz*. Understanding Zen is just as easy. Discovering the Zen of Oz can help you realize the higher purpose and pure potential of your life. Putting these ten spiritual lessons from over the rainbow into practice can help put you in dynamic harmony with the creative energy of the universe. They can help you discover your spiritual Self and fulfill your dreams. The journey down the Yellow Brick Road can miraculously make your life more glorious and joyful in every way—once you discover the keen Zen philosophy hidden within.

And this "kindly philosophy," as we shall see, is undoubtedly why *The Wizard of Oz* is one of the most beloved movies of all time.

To Oz!

—Joey Green

トト、もうカンザスじゃないよ

ONE

WE'RE NOT IN KANSAS ANYMORE

YOUR HAPPINESS IS DETERMINED BY YOUR karma. You have probably heard the saying, "What goes around comes around." That's the law of karma. Sir Isaac Newton put it this way, "For every action there is an equal and opposite reaction." The Bible puts it this way, "Whatever you sow, so shall you reap." In other words, every action, good or bad, causes a reaction. Good causes good; bad causes bad. It is the simple law of cause and effect. Every choice you make has a consequence, whether or not you make that choice consciously.

The choices Dorothy makes in Kansas turn her life bleak and gray, until it spins out of control like a tornado. This is a perfect example of bad karma. Dorothy runs home to tell Aunt Em and Uncle Henry that mean old Miss Gulch hit Toto with a rake and threatened to involve the Sheriff merely because the dog "gets into her garden and chases her nasty old cat every day."

But Aunt Em and Uncle Henry don't seem to care.

"Don't bother us now, honey," insists Uncle Henry, as he and Aunt Em take small chicks from the incubator and put them quickly under hens in nearby crates. "This old incubator's gone bad, and we're likely to lose a lot of our chicks."

But could there be something deeper going on here? Could the broken incubator really be Aunt Em and Uncle Henry's dysfunctional home, where Dorothy is ignored? The incubator has gone bad all right, and the chick Aunt Em and Uncle Henry are about to lose is their niece Dorothy.

Dorothy's Kansas is a bleak, gloomy, gray place because it is missing the love that would otherwise color her world if she were not an orphan. We never learn how Dorothy's parents died, but their deaths obviously left a vacuum in her life. Dorothy desperately yearns for Aunt Em's love as a replacement for the love of the mother she sorely misses. But Aunt Em isn't capable of taking the place of Dorothy's mother. She treats her niece as a nuisance and leaves her alone to work out her own problems.

"Now, Dorothy dear—stop imagining things," admonishes Aunt Em. "You always get yourself into a fret over nothing. Now you just help us out today and find yourself a place where you won't get into any trouble." Aunt Em doesn't nurture her adopted niece. She doesn't invite her to help with the farm work or include her in the family. Instead, she ridicules Dorothy for having a runaway imagination, ignores her pleas for help, tells her to get lost. Yet Aunt Em has plenty of time to prepare and serve crullers to the hired help.

"If happy little bluebirds fly over the rainbow, why, oh why, can't I?" laments Dorothy, longing for escape from the depressed Kansas farm. She seeks a nurturing environment where the dreams that she dares to dream really do come true. Dorothy dreams of a more affectionate and compassionate home. The rainbow, the only beauty Dorothy knows, represents the love she seeks to color her world.

In the meantime, Dorothy, a generous child with a heart full of love, focuses all her affection on her dog. In Dorothy's mind, only Toto loves her unconditionally, giving her a taste of the affection and companionship she craves.

Why then does Dorothy endanger Toto's life by letting him run through Miss Gulch's garden? Why pick on a mean-spirited, power-hungry old maid who carries her emotional baggage in a picnic basket strapped to the back of her bicycle?

Of course, the most obvious reason is to make Uncle Henry and Aunt Em take notice. When we find ourselves neglected by Aunt Em and Uncle Henry, when no one at home seems to have time for us, we subconsciously find a way to get their attention—usually by letting Toto run through Miss Gulch's garden.

When you choose to take actions that torment others and sow the seeds of unhappiness, the consequence of your karma is your own misery and failure. When you choose to take actions that nourish joy and love, the fruit of your karma is your own fulfillment and happiness.

The only way to rise above karma is to become aware of the unconscious choices you are constantly making. If Aunt Em and Uncle Henry do not treat you as their own child, you could choose to feel hurt and rejected. You could also choose to let it go. Either way, it's completely your choice. If, like Dorothy, you choose to feel hurt and rejected, you might then choose to break into a heartwarming song about some imaginary place over the rainbow where "troubles melt like lemon drops, away above the chimney tops." Or you might choose to let this hurt and rejection fester into anger and hostility. You might then choose to vent your anger and hostility by tormenting Miss Gulch. You may think that Aunt Em and Uncle Henry triggered your reaction. But whenever you impulsively react to something, you are actually choosing to respond that way. Your decision to react impulsively is simply an *unconscious* choice.

Hunk, one of the farmhands, tries to get Dorothy to step back and witness her unconscious choices. "When you come home, don't go by Miss Gulch's place," he tells her. "Then Toto won't get in her garden, and you won't get in no trouble, see?"

But Dorothy obviously wants to get into trouble.

When Miss Gulch arrives at the door with an order from the Sheriff to seize Toto, Dorothy gets more attention than she ever bargained for—only to learn that her aunt and uncle are spineless cowards, powerless and unwilling to defy Miss Gulch. Only then does Dorothy truly realize the futility of her control drama. She has sacrificed Toto—the one thing she loves most—in a vain attempt to win maternal love from a woman who will never love her like a daughter.

When Toto escapes from Miss Gulch's basket and leaps back through Dorothy's bedroom window, Dorothy childishly runs away from home with her dog, not merely to save Toto's life, but to seek a way to color her gray existence.

Crossing a bridge over a "gulch," Dorothy and Toto happen upon a decorated wagon belonging to Professor Marvel, a kindhearted carnival fakir roasting hot dogs over an open fire. Professor Marvel, pretending to be clairvoyant, deduces that Dorothy has run away. "They don't understand you at home," he intuits. "They don't appreciate you. . . . You want to see other lands—big cities—big mountains—big oceans!" Awed, Dorothy replies, "Why, it's just like you could read what was inside of me!" Marvel, claiming to be "in tune with the infinite," consults with his crystal ball and convinces Dorothy that Aunt Em has fallen ill. Realizing how much she loves Aunt Em, Dorothy races home, only to get caught in a cyclone and locked out of the storm cellar by her aunt and uncle, once again left to work out her own problems.

If you get caught in a cyclone because you ran away from home to save your dog from being destroyed by the Sheriff because you let the dog run through a mean old maid's garden, you might want to stop and ask yourself, "What is the universe trying to tell me?" Maybe the message is that you should stop and think what compelled you to let your dog run through the mean old maid's garden in the first place. Maybe Dorothy is subconsciously afraid that her own loveless environment will eventually turn her into a hateful, bitter, sour-faced Miss Gulch. Maybe Dorothy is unconsciously waging a battle against the adult she's afraid of turning into. Maybe Dorothy should ask herself why she wants Aunt Em's love so desperately. Maybe Dorothy is continually setting herself up for rejection to punish herself for the death of her parents.

The cyclone becomes a physical manifestation of Dorothy Gale's inner struggle for self-awareness, the result of the "gale" winds storming through her psyche. Struggling against the wind, Dorothy enters the farmhouse, runs from room to room, stamps her foot on the locked storm cellar doors, then runs back into the house to her bedroom, where she gets hit in the head by a window blown off its hinges. When the twister finally drops the house,

Dorothy opens the front door and crosses yet another threshold.

"Toto, I have a feeling we're not in Kansas anymore" becomes the anguished cry of a young woman catapulted by bad Karma into an endless cycle of rebirth into the next moment. Dorothy is compelled to repeat her Kansas experience in Oz by angering yet another wicked individual, seeking the advice of three more friends, journeying down another road, and putting her trust in yet another carnival fakir masquerading as a wizard. To break free from this pattern, Dorothy must rise above her karma. Only when she understands why she has been obsessively seeking Aunt Em's love and resolves the subconscious conflict that prompted her to risk Toto's life—aligning herself with the Tao and discovering her true Self—can Dorothy take control of her life, color the bleak landscape of her psyche, and attain satori (the Zen experience of awakening).

The lesson is simple. You can avoid a nightmarish trip over the rainbow if you are consciously aware of your choices in Kansas. All you have to do is step back and observe the choices you make every moment.

Your choices mirror how deeply you know your true Self. If, like Dorothy, every choice you make stems from your insecurity over Aunt Em's love, then this is a reflection of insecurity as a major obstacle to your self-awareness. An abundance of love from Aunt Em will not make you whole. Only an intimate understanding of your true Self—fully embracing your higher nature—will bring you security, aligning you with ultimate Oneness and infinite creative power of the universe.

Whenever you face a choice, consider the consequences of that choice. Will the consequences nourish happiness? The innermost essence of your being—your soul, your true Self, your higher consciousness—will intrinsically know the right answer. That choice will create good karma. If, on the other hand, you find yourself struggling against the wind, you are working against the rhythms of the universe. You must discover your inner spark and let your true Self take control of your life. Otherwise, if you go through life making unconscious choices—unnecessarily walking past Miss Gulch's house, refusing to cope with Kansas, and running away from your problems—like Dorothy, you will have to deal with the karmic consequences.

ルビーのスリッパをぬがないように

TWO
NEVER LET THOSE RUBY SLIPPERS OFF YOUR FEET

You are born with an inner spark. This inner spark gives you a potentially radiant character and the capability of knowing, loving, and spiritually communing with the creative intelligence of the universe. You are endowed with infinite potential for goodness and greatness. You have the free will to discover your inner spark and your cosmic purpose or the free will to extinguish your inner spark.

The ruby slippers actually represent the inner spark within us all. In Dorothy's dream, Glinda, the Good Witch of the North, is Dorothy's mother. She travels in a pink bubble, reminiscent of the womb. She gives Dorothy the ruby slippers—made, incidentally, from the rarest and costliest of gemstones—a physical reminder of the value of Dorothy's inner spark, the breath of life. Then she watches over Dorothy from afar, like a spirit.

When Glinda tells Dorothy, "Never let those ruby slippers off your feet," she is actually telling Dorothy to never give up her passion, her individuality, her uniqueness, her spirit, her soul—in short, her inner spark.

Think about it. After Dorothy crash-lands in Munchkinland, Glinda explains that Dorothy's house landed on the Wicked Witch of the East, killing the tyrant who ruled Munchkinland. The Munchkins, relieved to discover that Dorothy isn't a witch at all, sing Dorothy's praises. Unfortunately, the Wicked Witch of the West, who shows up in an ominous cloud of red smoke, doesn't share the Munchkins' joy. "Who killed my sister?" she demands. "Who killed the Witch of the East? Was it *you?*"

"No, no—it was an accident," pleads Dorothy. "I didn't mean to kill anyone."

When the Wicked Witch of the West threatens to cause an accident too, Glinda diverts her attention. "Aren't you forgetting the ruby slippers?" she asks. The Wicked Witch races over to the fallen house to snatch the slippers from her dead sister's feet, but the ruby slippers suddenly vanish. Her sister's feet, clad in only black-and-white striped socks, quickly shrivel up under the house. Without her inner spark, she completely withers away.

Glinda points her wand at the ruby slippers, now on Dorothy's feet. "There they are," she tells the Wicked Witch of the West, "and there they'll stay."

"Give me back my slippers!" demands the Wicked Witch of the West. "I'm the only one who knows how to use them. They're of no use to you!"

"Keep tight inside of them," Glinda instructs Dorothy. "Their magic must be very powerful, or she wouldn't want them so badly."

Glinda pretends to know very little about the ruby slippers, but she obviously knows a lot more about their magical powers than she reveals. Otherwise, she would never bring them to the Wicked Witch's attention in the first place or magically whisk them onto Dorothy's feet. How much more does Glinda know about the ruby slippers' true nature? And why won't she share this information with Dorothy, a girl she obviously wishes to protect?

When Glinda disappears in her pink bubble, Dorothy is left to figure out the power of the ruby slippers for herself. All she knows is that the Wicked Witch is obsessed with obtaining them. We never learn why the Wicked Witch doesn't have a pair of sparkling red shoes like those worn by her dead sister. Maybe the Wicked Witch of the West was jealous of her sister. Maybe she needs the ruby slippers to overcome that unresolved sibling rivalry. Maybe that's their "magical" power. The fact that she cannot kill Dorothy as long as the Kansas girl is wearing the ruby slippers proves that the shoes are more than just an ordinary pair of sequined red high heels.

One thing is certain. The Wicked Witch of the West extinguished her inner spark long before Dorothy arrives in Oz, explaining why, as Glinda insists, she is much worse than her late sister. The Wicked Witch of the East may have been evil, but at least she still wore a physical reminder of her inner spark on her feet. Maybe that's why the Wicked Witch of the East did not subjugate the Munchkins as cruelly as her sister from the West suppresses the blue-faced Winged Monkeys and the green-faced, uniformed Winkies who guard her castle.

The Wicked Witch of the West wants the ruby slippers not so she can rekindle her own inner spark. She wants the ruby slippers so "my power will be the greatest in Oz!" Her hunger for power, however, is a sign of insecurity. What the Wicked Witch is really chasing after is security. But security does not come from power. Security comes from self-love—knowing your true essence, your cosmic purpose, the pure

potential of your spiritual being, not by controlling the lives of others. By choosing a life of
righteousness, you come closer to the creative
force of the universe, fanning the flames of your
inner spark. By choosing wickedness, you distance yourself from the creative force of the universe, extinguishing your inner spark.

Bitterly jealous of Dorothy's youthful, impas-
sioned, loving spirit, the Wicked Witch tries to
extinguish Dorothy's inner spark to make the
Kansas girl as lonely and miserable as she is. When
the Winged Monkeys bring Dorothy to the Witch's
castle, the Witch puts Toto in a basket, just like
the one used by Miss Gulch. She threatens to
have the Winged Monkeys drop the basket in
the river and drown Toto—unless Dorothy gives

her the ruby slippers. Just like vindictive Miss Gulch, the Wicked Witch of the West plans to destroy Toto to kill Dorothy's spirit.

Embittered people who have extinguished their own inner spark justify their miserable existence by trying to extinguish the inner spark in others. But when the Wicked Witch of the West reaches for the ruby slippers, "sparks" fly from the shoes, giving the green-skinned witch a well-deserved electric shock. "Fool that I am!" she yells, "I should have remembered! Those slippers will never come off . . . as long as you're alive!"

Life is filled with people trying to get you down in the same hole that they're in. Teachers, politicians, bosses, even parents and friends, may try to rob you of your integrity, your passion, your reputation, your spirit, your cosmic purpose. They're no better than the Wicked Witch of the West trying to steal Dorothy's ruby slippers. But they can never get those ruby slippers off your feet—unless you let them. All you need to do is heed Glinda's words of warning. Never let those ruby slippers off your feet.

After Dorothy throws a bucket of water at the Wicked Witch, accidentally liquidating her, everyone forgets about the ruby slippers—until the Wizard takes off in his hot-air balloon without Dorothy. Glinda floats down in her pink bubble and tells Dorothy, "You've always had the power to go back to Kansas."

"Then why didn't you tell her before?" demands the Scarecrow, failing to use his brain.

"Because she wouldn't have believed me," explains Glinda. "She had to learn it for herself." In other words, Dorothy had to discover her cosmic purpose, her intrinsic nature, her spiritual essence, on her own.

Dorothy agrees. "If I ever go looking for my heart's desire again, I won't look any further than my own backyard," she cryptically tells her friends, "because if it isn't there, I never really lost it to begin with."

The answers are within, not handed to you on a silver platter by a wizard or a witch. As Dorothy learns, discovering your cosmic purpose brings you home to your true nature, empowering you and your ruby slippers. And the way to discover your cosmic purpose, to achieve Oneness with your spiritual essence, is to follow the Yellow Brick Road.

黄色の石の道を進め

THREE

FOLLOW THE
YELLOW BRICK ROAD

THE UNIVERSE IS COMPOSED OF PURE ENERGY. On a subatomic level, you and everything around you is made up of energy. Your mind is in harmony with the infinite creative intelligence of the universe. This is the Oneness of the cosmos.

When the Munchkins urge their national heroine to follow the Yellow Brick Road, their simplistic street directions become an inspiring mantra:

Follow the Yellow Brick Road.
Follow the Yellow Brick Road.
Follow, Follow, Follow, Follow,
Follow the Yellow Brick Road.

The Munchkins are doing more than encouraging Dorothy to follow a path paved with the promise of golden opportunity. They're urging her to follow her true nature, to follow her instincts, in short, to align herself with the Tao and embrace her true Self so that everything her heart desires will come to her.

The Tao is the creative force of the universe. The Tao creates the world organically, spontaneously, and without effort. The word Tao is often translated as "the way" or "the path." It is the way of the world, the creative intelligence that shapes the world with an awe-inspiring skill far beyond our comprehension. When you align yourself with the Tao, you align yourself with the infinite potential of the universe.

The irony of Zen is that you cannot align yourself with the Tao by *attempting* to align yourself with the Tao. You don't have to work on being in harmony with the Tao. You are already in harmony with the Tao. When you allow your mind to function freely and naturally, without being self-conscious, you simply follow the Yellow Brick Road and go with the flow.

The *Hsin-hsin Ming,* a revered poem attributed to Zen sage Seng-ts'an, puts it best:

> *Follow your nature and accord with the*
> *Tao;*
> *Saunter along and stop worrying.*

When Glinda, the Good Witch of the North, floats down to Munchkinland, her first question to Dorothy is: "Are you a good witch or a bad witch?"

Taken aback, Dorothy responds, "I'm not a witch at all. Witches are old and ugly."

The Munchkins, hiding amidst the flowers, giggle.

"They're laughing," explains Glinda "because I *am* a witch."

"You *are?* Oh, I beg your pardon!" replies Dorothy, curtsying politely. "But I've never heard of a beautiful witch before."

"Only bad witches are ugly," explains Glinda.

If only bad witches are ugly, as Glinda insists, why then does Glinda ask Dorothy whether she is a good or a bad witch? Does Glinda consider Dorothy to be ugly? Or is Glinda talking about inner beauty and inner ugliness?

Before sending Dorothy on the long journey to seek the Wizard of Oz, Glinda asks her, "Did you bring your broomstick with you?"— once again implying that Dorothy is not only a witch, but a bad witch at that (since good witches like Glinda travel by way of a magic wand and pink bubble). Then again, we never meet a Witch of the South, who, for all we know, may very well be a good witch who travels by broomstick.

Why then does Glinda ask Dorothy whether she is a good witch or a bad witch in the first place? Could Glinda be planting this question in Dorothy's mind to give the young Kansas girl something to ponder while following the Yellow Brick Road? Are you good or evil? Are you selfish or unselfish?

Glinda plants the soul-searching question in Dorothy's mind and sends her skipping down the Yellow Brick Road so that Dorothy will align herself with the Tao, consciously connect with her higher Self, and find inner peace. Dorothy follows the Yellow Brick Road in search of something she never lost—her true Self. All she really needs is the brains, the heart, and the courage to let go and trust her natural, spontaneous instincts. Zen is when you don't force your true essence to shine through; it simply grows that way—spontaneously, easily, and effortlessly. As Zen sage Huang Po wrote in the *Ch'uan Hsin Fa Yao:* "When body and mind achieve spontaneity, the Tao is reached and cosmic intelligence can be understood."

Dorothy repeats strong positive statements to convince herself that her goal is real and possible, dispel any doubts she may have, and elevate her outlook on life. She sings "Follow the Yellow Brick Road" and "We're off to see the Wizard," positive affirmations that transform her attitudes and expectations, ultimately changing the reality she creates for herself.

Eventually, Dorothy reaches a poignant crossroad along the Yellow Brick Road. The

Yellow Brick Road isn't a clear-cut path. It forks and divides. "Now which way do we go?" she asks Toto.

"Pardon me," says the Scarecrow hanging from a pole, his arm pointing to the right, "That way is a very nice way."

"Who said that?" asks Dorothy. Toto barks at the Scarecrow, but Dorothy looks uneasily at her dog. "Don't be silly, Toto. Scarecrows don't talk."

"It's pleasant down that way, too," says the Scarecrow, now pointing to the left.

"That's funny," Dorothy tells Toto, oblivious to the fact that dogs can't talk either. "Wasn't he pointing the other way?"

"Of course, people do go both ways!" says the Scarecrow, crossing his arms to point in both directions.

Choosing is absurd. It doesn't really matter which fork in the road Dorothy takes. As long as she follows the Yellow Brick Road, all the roads lead to self-actualization. If Dorothy, Toto, and the Scarecrow go one way, they will meet the Tin Man and the Cowardly Lion. If they take the other route, they will undoubtedly affect the lives of others as they go with the flow, enjoy the here and now, and guide themselves consciously toward the Emerald City. As Zen poet Seng-t'san put it in the opening words of the *Hsin-hsin Ming*:

> *The perfect Way is without difficulty,*
> *Save that it avoids picking and choosing.*

The decisions life throws in your path aren't always as important as they may seem. Should you take the scenic route or the highway? Should you go to this college or that college? Should you take the job or not take the job? The decisions themselves are immaterial. What matters is that you make the choice, that you have the courage to move forward. If you are paralyzed by indecision, you become stagnant, dull, lifeless— just like the Scarecrow stuck on his pole. If you turn around and race back to the safety and security of Munchkinland, you regress, degenerate, deteriorate. Only by moving forward, only by braving the unknown, experiencing uncertainty, and opening yourself up to the infinite possibilities, do you realize your dreams, find your heart's desire, and discover freedom and fulfillment. When you step into the unknown, you are on the right path—the road less traveled. Enjoy every moment of the journey. As Robert Louis Stevenson wrote in *El Dorado:* "To travel hopefully is a better thing than to arrive."

Besides, you never travel the Yellow Brick Road alone. Dorothy's passion for self-discovery becomes contagious. She inspires the Scarecrow, the Tin Man, the Cowardly Lion, and even the Wizard himself to join her quest for self-fulfillment and unblock the barriers they have created to the naturally harmonious, abundant, and loving flow of the universe.

The Scarecrow, the Tin Man, and the Cowardly Lion all "dwell" by the side of the Yellow Brick Road, yearning to fill a void in their lives, yet failing to venture out on the Yellow Brick Road—until Dorothy comes along.

The Scarecrow, nailed to a post, cannot go anywhere, representing those people in life who let others hold them back from realizing their dreams and aspirations.

The Tin Man, having rusted solid, is also im-mobilized. But before he rusted in place a year earlier, the Tin Man could have journeyed up the Yellow Brick Road—unless he needed to stand still for a year to delve into his troubled soul and come to the realization that he is "all hollow," as he proclaims. The Tin Man represents a second group of soul-searchers: those paralyzed by indecisiveness.

The Cowardly Lion could have journeyed up the Yellow Brick Road any time he wished, representing yet a third group of individuals: those who lack the courage to make the spiritual journey alone.

Dorothy inspires her comrades by pointing out that they have nothing to lose but their unhappiness.

"Do you think if I went with you, the Wizard would give me some brains?" asks the Scarecrow.

"I couldn't say," admits Dorothy. "But even if he didn't, you'd be no worse off than you are now."

If you are discontented, Dorothy tells us, don't wallow in self-pity. Set a goal. Imagine yourself reaching that goal, picture it often, and give it lots of positive energy. Clear your mind of all negative thoughts and let your energy flow into the universe for the good of yourself and others.

Dorothy visualizes a Wizard at the end of the Yellow Brick Road who will send her back to Kansas. She focuses on the idea, giving it positive energy, convinced that the mental image is possible. As she follows the Yellow Brick Road, she never stops seeing herself being sent home when she reaches the Wizard.

You attract into your life whatever you picture most vividly. If you are afraid and insecure, you tend to create bad karma and attract wicked witches into your life. If you have a positive attitude and visualize spiritual fulfillment you will meet a Scarecrow, Tin Man, and Cowardly Lion, who will help you reach Oz.

The universe works through the dynamic exchange of energy. Energy circulates in a constant give-and-take. Call it whatever you want: Yin-Yang, karma, Tao, poetic justice. The more you give, the more you receive. Dorothy gives the Scarecrow, the Tin Man, and the Cowardly Lion hope and love. They return her love ten-fold, risking their lives to rescue her from the Wicked Witch's castle.

Of course, the Yellow Brick Road is not without potholes. The road may lead through an orchard of talking trees that throw apples at you. The road may take you through a dark forest filled with lions and tigers and bears. Or you may walk through a field of deadly poppies that knock you unconscious. The Yellow Brick Road may even seem to be going in the opposite direction of the Emerald City. But if you go with the flow, following the path of least resistance, the universe will unfold perfectly.

Do not hold onto your goal too tightly. If the Wizard accidentally takes off in his hot-air balloon without you, the universe may be trying to show you something better. When Dorothy lets go and connects with her inner essence, she ultimately realizes she has all the love she needs within her own heart to be at home with herself.

Aligning yourself with the Tao is more than just wishful thinking. It means following the

Yellow Brick Road toward your goal, while holding onto that goal loosely and going with the flow. Dorothy does not simply take up residence in Munchkinland and wait for another cyclone to whisk her and Toto back to Kansas. She journeys down the Yellow Brick Road, while staying open to the harmonious forces in the universe that will unfold before her. No matter which fork she takes, no matter who her companions are, no matter what obstacles are placed in her path, Dorothy will ultimately be returned to Kansas once she puts herself in tune with the creative energy of the universe. Along the way, she just happens to free the Munchkins from the Wicked Witch of the East; inspire the Scarecrow, the Tin Man, and the Cowardly Lion to find their true Selves; emancipate the Winkie Guards and the Winged Monkeys from the Wicked Witch of the West; liberate the people of the Emerald City from the Wizard's benevolent dictatorship; and free the Wizard himself from his self-imposed seclusion.

The challenge of opening the channels to your higher Self and to the forces of the universe may seem overwhelming at first, but all you need to do is listen to what the Munchkins are really saying—namely to follow the Yellow Brick Road one brick at a time. As the ancient Zen saying puts it, "A journey of a thousand miles begins with one step."

脳のないヤツほどよくしゃべる

FOUR

SOME PEOPLE
WITHOUT BRAINS
DO AN AWFUL LOT
OF TALKING

Those who know don't talk.
Those who talk don't know.
—*Tao Tê Ching*

YOUR SPIRITUAL ESSENCE IS PURE CONSCIOUS-ness. The deeper you know your true Self, the closer you align yourself with the pure potential and total Oneness of the universe. Discover your radiant inner being and you unleash the pure potential of your spiritual essence.

Suppose, like the Scarecrow, you're stuck in a job far beneath your level of intelligence. You're nailed to a pole in the middle of a cornfield. Your only responsibility is to scare crows. You're smart enough to handle the job, but your heart just isn't in it. Your enthusiasm for the job quickly wanes. Instead of inspiring you, the job becomes a humiliating reminder of your failure. No matter how smart you really are, you subconsciously convince yourself that you can't be all that bright if you're stuck in a cornfield scaring crows. You start to denigrate yourself until you destroy your self-esteem. You convince yourself that you can't scare a crow because you don't have a brain. The truth is: You're just too smart for such a menial job. Your passion lies in greater intellectual pursuits. Deep down in your soul you know you have to get off that pole, discover your true essence, and unleash your infinite potential.

For someone who insists he doesn't have a brain, the Scarecrow has been giving an awful lot of thought to what he would think about if he did have one. "I'd think of things I never thunk before," he reveals, "and then I'd sit and think some more." As a conscious being, the only thing you need to find happiness is to perceive clearly who you are. Being upset about what you don't have wastes what you do have. The very fact that the Scarecrow craves wisdom means he already has smarts. What he really yearns for is higher consciousness, enlightenment, nirvana.

When the Scarecrow asks Dorothy if he can accompany her to the Emerald City to ask the Wizard for some brains, Dorothy warns him against it. "I've got a witch mad at me," explains Dorothy, "and you might get into trouble."

"Witch? Hmph. I'm not afraid of a witch," insists the Scarecrow. "I'm not afraid of anything—except a lighted match. . . . But I'd face a whole box of them for the chance of getting some brains."

The Scarecrow's head may be filled with straw, but he also happens to echo the most profound metaphysical insights of the world's greatest philosophical thinkers. The French philosopher Jean-Paul Sartre proclaimed, "Existence precedes essence." In other words, you exist whether or not you have discovered your true

Self, your cosmic purpose, your existential authenticity. The Scarecrow, however, is willing to risk his existence to discover his essence. He would face a whole box of matches for the chance to reach his pure potential. The Greek philosopher Plato urged his disciples to "Know thyself." The Scarecrow, convinced he doesn't have a brain (yet determined to "know himself"), unwittingly embraces Plato's tenet that "A life unexamined is not worth living." The lesson? If you leave your essence unexamined, you are no better than a man made from straw. This is also an essential Zen belief. The *Tao Te Ching* puts it this way:

> *Knowing others is intelligence;*
> *Knowing yourself is true wisdom.*
> *Mastering others is strength;*
> *Mastering yourself is true power.*

As Dorothy and her companions nervously follow the Yellow Brick Road through a dark and creepy forest, the Scarecrow says, "Of course, I don't know, but I think it'll get darker before it gets lighter." The Scarecrow is actually offering a keen philosophical insight: An ontological confrontation with nothingness precedes the discovery of one's existential authenticity. Or as the *Tao Te Ching* sums it up so simply: "The path into the light seems dark." How could the brainless Scarecrow possibly be on the same wavelength as the greatest Zen thinkers?

Nature's intelligence flows freely and effortlessly. When you are in harmony with the creative intelligence of the cosmos, when you know your true Self, you can harness the pure potential of the universe. But before you can know your true Self, you must free yourself from your insecurities, your past conditioning, your guilt trips, your compulsions to control others, your need for approval. Carrying around all this old baggage wastes your energy. If you have been stuck on a pole in the middle of a cornfield with crows pecking at you, let it go. Free that energy, rechannel it, allow it to manifest itself in a more meaningful way. Accept things as they are—here and now.

Your true Self is your radiant inner being, your spirit, your higher consciousness, your soul.

It isn't afraid of anything—not even a lighted match. It is pure awareness, your direct connection to the Tao—the totally spontaneous creative force of the universe. The Tao does everything by doing nothing. Align yourself with it—let your talents flow easily, effortlessly—and you unleash your abundant ingenuity and natural creative power. To acquire anything you desire, simply give up your attachment to the outcome. By keeping your attention in the here and now, everything you wish will spontaneously flow from the Tao within you.

When the Scarecrow craves intelligence, it escapes him. When the Scarecrow lets go of his preoccupation with obtaining brains, he becomes a quick-thinking problem solver. Lao-tzu, the Zen philosopher and poet, wrote: "Free from desire, you realize the mystery." When the Scarecrow accepts the here and now, every obstacle he encounters becomes an opportunity in disguise:

- Dorothy can't figure out how to get him down from his pole, but the Scarecrow spontaneously proposes "If you'll just bend the nail down in the back, maybe I'll slip off."

- When the talking apple trees refuse to give their apples to Dorothy, the Scarecrow instinctively uses reverse psychology to provoke the trees to throw their apples at him and Dorothy.

- When the Doorman to the Emerald City asks Dorothy to prove that the Good Witch of the North sent her to see the Wizard, the Scarecrow impulsively points to the most persuasive evidence: "She's wearing the ruby slippers she gave her!"

- After the Scarecrow, the Tin Man, and the Cowardly Lion follow Toto to the castle of the Wicked Witch, the Scarecrow, unconsciously aligned with the Tao, proposes that they change into the guards' uniforms and infiltrate the castle by following the Winkie Guards as they march over the drawbridge.

- When the Witch's guards, armed with spears, close in on Dorothy and her friends, the Scarecrow instinctively jerks the Tin Man's ax to cut a nearby rope to the huge flaming chandelier hanging overhead falls on the guards—unaware that his ingenious problem-solving abilities easily outshine those of his companions.

The Scarecrow is like the highly intelligent individual, who, unable to afford college (or nailed to a metaphorical pole), feels inferior to anyone with a degree. As the Wizard tells him: "Back where I come from, we have universities, seats of great learning—where men go to become great thinkers, and when they come out, they think deep thoughts—and with no more brains than you have—but they have one thing you haven't got! A diploma!"

The Scarecrow should be an example to anyone who feels intellectually inadequate: You're smarter than you think. When you trust the power of your true Self, you have no need to impress others, to seek approval, to do "an awful lot of talking." You are at home with yourself and at one with the Tao.

The moment the Wizard bestows the honorary degree of Th.D. (Doctor of Thinkology) upon the Scarecrow, the Scarecrow points to his head and self-consciously recites what he thinks to be the Isosceles Triangle Theorem: "The sum of the square root of any two sides of an isosceles triangle is equal to the square root of the remaining side." But the Scarecrow is just plain wrong. Trying to impress others, he confuses the Isosceles Triangle Theorem with the Pythagorean Theorem and becomes someone without a brain doing an awful lot of talking. What he means to say is: "The square of the hypotenuse of a right triangle equals the sum of the squares of the remaining two sides." By self-consciously trying to use his brain, the Scarecrow puts himself out of sync with the Tao and prevents his natural creative power from flowing easily and effortlessly. Remaining aligned with the Tao means remaining *naturally* natural and *spontaneously* spontaneous. As Lao-tzu confirmed:

> *When you look for it, there is nothing*
> *to see.*
> *When you listen for it, there is nothing*
> *to hear.*
> *When you use it, it is inexhaustible.*

FIVE

HEARTS WILL NEVER BE PRACTICAL UNTIL THEY CAN BE MADE UNBREAKABLE

Only by doing good for others can you attain your own good. By giving to others you actually help yourself. It is not the recipient who is blessed, it is the giver. By simply putting the goodness within you to work for others, by nurturing love for love's sake, by giving of yourself unselfishly, the grace of the cosmos will flow back to you.

After the Wizard gives the Tin Man a huge heart-shaped watch and chain, he urges his sentimental friend to remember that "a heart is judged not by how much you love, but by how much you are loved by others."

But what exactly does the Wizard mean?

Is the Wizard saying that a good-deed-doer who is not loved by others does not really have a heart? What about the philanthropist who donates huge sums of money to charity anonymously and never receives any recognition? Does he have a smaller heart than the egotist who gives to charity to have a building named after himself? Is public opinion really an accurate barometer by which to judge a person's heart? The citizens of the Emerald City love the Wizard of Oz, but does that mean he has a bigger heart than the Tin Man, who is loved only by Dorothy, the Scarecrow, and the Cowardly Lion?

The Wizard's seemingly simple statement is actually a *koan*. In Zen, a koan is a "riddle" with no apparent meaning. A Zen master puts a koan before a student to train the mind to obtain satori (the Zen experience of awakening) in a sudden flash. A student may spend a split second or several years contemplating the meaning of a koan.

The koan is: Is a heart judged by how deeply you are loved by others? Or is the depth of your love the true measure of a heart?

How deeply you are loved by others does reveal the depth and sincerity of your love for them. No one loves the Wicked Witch of the West, for instance, because she doesn't have a smidgen of love for anyone. She doesn't even mourn the death of her sister, the Wicked Witch of the East; instead, she wants her shoes. She also wants to kill Dorothy, not to avenge her sister's death, but rather to eliminate any possible threat to her plans to seize control over the entire Land of Oz. Her motives are selfish and egocentric. She has no heart. She loves no one and no one loves her in return.

The Wizard, on the other hand, is loved by the citizens of the Emerald City—as long as he protects them from the Wicked Witch of the West. But the Wizard's love for the citizenry of the Emerald City is not genuine. Yes, he protects the Emerald City, but only so he can remain in power. Yes, he agrees to grant the requests of Dorothy and her friends, but only if they bring back the broomstick of the Wicked Witch. His love is conditional and insincere. He has a heart only by virtue of the fact that he is loved by others. He would be loved much more deeply if he were not such a humbug.

How much you are loved by others is equal to how deeply you love. If your love for others is selfless, you are much more deeply loved than a person whose love is selfish and motivated by greed. Love expands. Selfishness contracts. The more you expand and feel for others, the more you purify your own heart, aligning yourself with the Oneness of all things. But having a heart requires more than compassion. It is not enough to pity someone. It is necessary to serve others with unselfish love.

Immediately after Dorothy and the Scarecrow discover the Tin Man rusted in the woods and oil his joints, the Tin Man urges them to bang on his chest. The Scarecrow admires the resulting echo, but the Tin Man sadly explains that the tinsmith forgot to give him a heart and laments that he is "all hollow"—a curious bow to T. S. Eliot's renowned poem "The Hollow Men":

We are the hollow men
We are the stuffed men
Leaning together
Headpiece filled with straw.

The subtle reference brilliantly alludes to the many people who never seek or heed their inner essence and consequently fail to grasp their true potential, never letting their lives touch anyone in a positive way. The distraught Tin Man, on the other hand, longs to be "tender," "gentle," "and awful sentimental":

When a man's an empty kettle
He should be on his mettle
And yet I'm torn apart
Just because I'm presumin'
That I could be kind-a human
If I only had a heart.

Moments later, the Wicked Witch appears, perched on the roof of the Tin Man's cottage. She threatens to stuff a mattress with the Scarecrow and use the Tin Man for a beehive unless the two fine gentlemen stay away from Dorothy and stop helping her along. She then throws a ball of fire at the Scarecrow. The Tin Man slams his tin hat down on the fireball to extinguish it—a purely selfless act of loving kindness.

The Scarecrow insists that he will get Dorothy to the Wizard whether he gets a brain or not. The Tin Man, having just met the two soul seekers, chimes in, insisting that he'll get Dorothy to the Wizard whether he gets a heart or not. The Tin Man's altruism proves he already has an enormous heart. His willingness to sacrifice his life for Dorothy is indeed the ultimate good deed—an act of selfless love.

If you want to be blessed with a heart, you must give with your heart. You have probably heard the saying "Give and you shall receive." Helping others get what they want is the easiest way to get what you want. When you give from your heart, sympathetically, unconditionally, constantly, and without expecting anything in return, you receive happiness in abundance. Love is a life force that must continue circulating. To keep that energy coming to you, you must keep love in perpetual motion.

It is vitally important, however, that you make certain the intention behind your giving is selfless. You cannot have an ulterior motive. You cannot be trying to manipulate anyone. You cannot be trying to create indebtedness. Your goal should always be to create happiness for its own sake. The most precious gifts you can give are not material gifts. The most precious gifts you can give are spiritual: compassion, sympathy, countenance, affection, appreciation, and love. These are the gifts that the Tin Man unwittingly, unconsciously, and instinctively gives to everyone he meets.

Unfortunately, love is a double-edged sword. When you love someone, when you feel for the well-being of others, your heart is easily broken—particularly when you see someone you love being hurt. The overly sympathetic Tin Man cries when his companions fall victim to the Witch's poppy field. When the Scarecrow, the Tin Man, and the Cowardly Lion follow Toto back to the Witch's castle, the Tin Man, realizing Dorothy is being held prisoner inside that awful place, is brought to tears. When the Tin Man cries, when his feelings overpower him, he rusts. Being overly sensitive—being attached—is paralyzing. Love must be allowed to flow, to strengthen, to empower you to serve others. If you allow love to stop flowing, to remain stagnant, to bottle up inside you and fester, you interrupt the flow of energy in the universe.

The heartbroken Tin Man remains convinced he does not have a heart, failing to see his heartache as heartfelt emotion. He gives love so selflessly and instinctively that he isn't even aware of how much love he gives. Without knowing it, the Tin Man touches, in a positive way, the lives of nearly everyone he meets. His generosity is so genuine, he doesn't even realize that he does nothing all day but perform acts of loving kindness. And that, as the Wizard insists, is what having a heart is all about. Not until Dorothy says goodbye does the Tin Man suddenly realize he will no longer be able to receive the joy of giving love to Dorothy. The realization makes him feel terribly hollow once more. "Now I know I have a heart," he laments, "because it's breaking."

A heart is indeed judged by how much you are loved by others. But how much you are loved by others is determined by how much you love. In other words, the love, sympathy, appreciation, compassion, countenance, and affection you receive are in direct proportion to the love, sympathy, appreciation, compassion, countenance, and affection you give. The Wizard is essentially telling the Tin Man the same thing Zen poets have been telling the world for centuries: "What goes around comes around."

森の王様になったら

SIX

IF I WERE KING

OF THE FOREST

Your true self—your spiritual essence, your inner spark, your intrinsic nature—does not fear any challenge. It is completely fearless. It is neither inferior nor superior to anyone. Your true Self is pure consciousness, unencumbered by insecurity, apprehension, external circumstances, or the need for approval or control. This pure consciousness can do anything. It is invincible.

Unfortunately, our thinking and our behavior, shackled by the material world, is generally based on fear. When the Lion first leaps from the forest, he takes a boxer's stance and starts name-calling, labeling the Tin Man a "shivering junk-yard" and the Scarecrow a "lopsided bag of hay." Unable to provoke a fight with the Scarecrow or the Tin Man, the Lion chases after Toto, prompting Dorothy to slap the Lion on the nose. When the Lion starts crying, Dorothy explains, "Well, naturally when you go around picking on things weaker than you are—why, you're nothing but a great big coward!"

Dorothy encounters two other cowards in the Land of Oz who go around picking on things weaker than they are—the Wizard and the Wicked Witch of the West. Just like the Cowardly Lion, the Wizard picks on Dorothy and her companions the moment they set foot on his turf. He too immediately resorts to name-calling. He labels the Tin Man a "clanking, clattering collection of caliginous junk" and the Scarecrow "a billowing bale of bovine fodder." The Wicked Witch of the West threatens to stuff a mattress with the Scarecrow and make a bee-hive out of the Tin Man, and then, just like the

Cowardly Lion, proceeds to pick on Dorothy's "mangy little dog."

Cowards feel compelled to conquer other people to compensate for the fact that they have not conquered themselves. The Wizard controls the Emerald City but hides behind a curtain, afraid to face the populace. In Kansas, Miss Gulch owns half the county (yet still rides a bicycle) and longs to control the other half. In Oz, the Wicked Witch of the West controls half of the land of Oz and also aspires to control the rest of it. Why? All relationships reflect your relationship with yourself. If you feel the need to control other people, what you really need is to control yourself.

The Lion yearns to be king of the forest, but what he really craves is to be king over himself. Being crowned king of the forest, being acclaimed "Oz, the First Wizard deluxe," or gaining the ruby slippers to achieve the greatest power in Oz will not fill this void in your existence. Only discovering your true Self will start you on the path toward spiritual fulfillment. The Lion clearly wants to be king of the forest for the wrong reasons:

As I'd click my heel,
All the trees would kneel,
And the mountains bow,
And the bulls kowtow,
And the sparrow would take wing
If I . . . if I were King.
Each rabbit would show respect to me.
The chipmunks genuflect to me.
Though my tail would lash,
I would show compash
For every underling
If I . . . if I were King.

Unfortunately, if—like the Lion—you need to subjugate others to compensate for your insecurities, you become a cruel and selfish leader—just like the Witch and the Wizard. When you are king over yourself, you become a compassionate and caring leader—just like Glinda, the Good Witch of the North. The *Tao Te Ching* puts it this way: "He who has power over others cannot empower himself."

When you intimately know your true Self, you will never feel a need to "command each thing, be it fish or fowl, with a *woof!* and a *woof!* and royal growl." Instead, you will realize that true power stems from power over yourself—the ability to trust your intrinsic nature and let its pure potential flow effortlessly and abundantly.

When Dorothy asks to see the Wizard of Oz, the Guard to the Palace firmly replies, "Orders are: Nobody can see the Great Oz, not nobody, not nohow!" Moments later, while the Lion shares his dream of being king of the forest, Dorothy asks him whether he would be afraid of anything. The Lion, mimicking the Guard, responds, "Not nobody, not nohow!" He erroneously believes he has to be a bully. When asked if he'd be afraid of a hippopotamus, the Lion insists, "Why, I'd thrash him from top to bottomus." If he meets an elephant, the Lion vows, "I'll wrap him up in cellophant." The Lion is foolishly confusing courage with intimidation. A courageous individual does not resort to intimidation. Only a bully uses intimidation. Only a bully is habitually cruel to smaller or weaker people.

While singing about his desire to be king of the forest, the Lion poses a series of questions that have obviously plagued his troubled soul:

- "What makes the elephant charge his tusk in the misty mist or the dusky dusk?"
- "What makes the muskrat guard his musk?"
- "What makes the Hottentot so hot?"
- "What puts the 'ape' in apricot?"
- "What have they got that I ain't got?"

But the Lion fails to ask the most important question of all: Why do the elephant, the muskrat, the Hottentot, and the apricot all possess the courage he sorely lacks?

Like the Wicked Witch of the West and the Wizard, the Lion yearns for power merely to validate himself, not to express a unique talent for leadership or to serve his fellow creatures. To truly be king of the forest, you must cast away your need for power and control. You must get in touch with your spiritual essence. You must discover your higher Self, your innate grandeur, your purpose in life. The inner spark deep within your soul has taken a body for a cosmic purpose, and you must discover what that purpose is. You must ask yourself what your unique talents are. Once you have discovered the talents that make you special—the things you love to do, your passion—ask yourself, "How can I use my unique talents to help others?" When you seek your higher Self, when you discover your passion, and when you strive to put your unique talents to work for the benefit of humanity, courage miraculously flows with effortless ease and you commune with the genius of the universal intelligence. Only then will you experience the ecstacy of existence.

As the four travelers walk down the high palace corridor toward the Wizard's throne room, the Cowardly Lion, twiddling his tail nervously, suddenly wails in pain. "Somebody pulled my tail," he bawls. The Scarecrow points out, "You did it yourself." This single moment succinctly encapsulates a profound Zen teaching. As the great master Lao-tsu wrote, "There is no greater illusion than fear." Franklin Delano Roosevelt put it this way: "The only thing we have to fear is fear itself."

On a deeper level, the Cowardly Lion may be afraid to unleash the pure potential of his true Self. "I'm afraid there's no denyin' I'm just a dandelion," he gaily admits, gesturing with a decidedly limp wrist, possibly insinuating that his sexual orientation is "a fate I don't deserve." At the Wash & Brush Up Co. in the Emerald City, the Lion gets a permanent crowned with a large red bow, and while claiming to have "a certain air of savoir faire" lets his wrist go limp again. When the Guard refuses to announce the four travelers to the Wizard, the Lion effeminately laments, "And I got a permanent just for the occasion." With a noticeably feminine flair, the Cowardly Lion sings:

> *If I were King of the Forest,*
> *Not Queen, not Duke, not Prince,*
> *My regal robes of the forest,*
> *Would be satin, not cotton, not chintz.*

He unnecessarily rules out the possibility of being Queen, but then goes to curious lengths to delicately specify his refined taste in fabrics. If the Lion does indeed lack the courage to accept his sexual orientation and come out of the closet, he must muster the inner strength to embrace his true Self—if he ever wishes to find spiritual freedom and fulfillment. Otherwise, shackled by fear, the Lion prevents himself from becoming conscious of his innate grandeur (just like Miss Gulch, who may very well be a victim of her own repressed sexuality).

In the meantime, the Lion foolishly clings to negative thoughts, undermining his self-confidence and reinforcing his cowardice. As the four travelers march through the Haunted Forest toward the Witch's Castle, the Lion self-destructively chants a superstitious mantra:

> *I do believe in spooks.*
> *I do believe in spooks.*
> *I do, I do, I do, I do, I do,*
> *I do believe in spooks.*

Instead, the Lion should use a positive affirmation to conquer his fear—the same way Dorothy, the Scarecrow, and the Tin Man start chanting "Lions and tigers and bears—oh my!" to propel themselves along the Yellow Brick Road when it enters a dark and eerie forest.

How then does the Lion find his courage? When the Lion discovers that Dorothy is being held prisoner in the Witch's Castle, his love for Dorothy overpowers all his fears. In a flash, the

Lion discovers his higher Self, recognizes his unique talent, and impulsively decides to use his strengths to save Dorothy. "All right," the Lion announces, "I'll go in there for Dorothy— Wicked Witch or no Wicked Witch—guards or no guards—I'll tear 'em apart! I may not come out alive, but I'm going in there!" As the Zen sage Lao-tzu wrote: "Because of deep love, one is courageous."

"There's only one thing I want you fellas to do," requests the Lion.

"What's that?" ask the Scarecrow and Tin Man.

"Talk me out of it."

When the triumphant foursome return with the Witch's broomstick, the Wizard brazenly orders them to go away and come back the following day. The Lion, having found his true Self, has no hesitation confronting the Wizard. When the humbled Wizard eventually presents the Lion with the Triple Cross "for meritorious conduct, extraordinary valor, conspicuous bravery against wicked witches," he claims that the Lion is mere- ly "under the unfortunate delusion that simply because you run away from danger, you have no courage." The Wizard, with Zen-like clarity, confides, "You're confusing courage with wisdom."

Before leaving the Emerald City aboard his hot-air balloon, the Wizard appoints the Scarecrow ruler of Oz, to be assisted by the Tin Man and the Lion. The Lion, having yearned to be king of the forest, accepts a position of even greater significance, allowing him to use his newfound courage to serve his fellow creatures on a more grandiose scale. The message is clear. If you, like the Lion, discover your true Self and your purpose in life, you too can access the infinite potential of the cosmos, freeing yourself to experience life as a miraculous expression of love. All it takes is a little courage.

あきらめろ ドロシー

SEVEN

SURRENDER DOROTHY

YOUR HEART'S DESIRE IS YOUR DESTINY. BUT to fulfill that destiny, you must first give up your attachment to the outcome. You don't give up your *intention* to realize your desire. You simply detach yourself from the result. In other words, you surrender to the creative intelligence of the cosmic nexus and allow it to unfold before you.

When the Wicked Witch of the West writes the words "Surrender Dorothy" in black smoke in the sky over the Emerald City, Dorothy is not about to give up her burning desire to return to Kansas. The Witch may be her sworn enemy, but even your worst enemy has something to teach you. Ironically, the Witch, ruthlessly attached to her own twisted desire to gain the ruby slippers, inadvertently teaches Dorothy how to detach herself from her own burning desire.

Of course, Dorothy surrenders moments after she arrives in Munchkinland. Back in Kansas, Dorothy longed to journey over the rainbow to a place where the dreams that she dares to dream really do come true. The tornado seemed to be the answer to Dorothy's prayers. It whisked her over the rainbow to a place far away from dreary, desolate Kansas.

Now Dorothy can stay in Technicolor Munchkinland forever. Having accidentally killed the Wicked Witch of the East, she is welcomed with open arms as a national heroine. She turns down the opportunity to be classified as a good witch or a bad witch, but still the Munchkins, convinced she has fallen from a star called Kansas, promise to glorify her name and make a bust of her in their Hall of Fame. The Mayor of the Munchkin

City welcomes her most regally, as do the Lullaby League and the Lollipop Guild, and she's given the equivalent of a ticker-tape parade in a pony-driven carriage. Dorothy is obviously more than welcome to make Munchkinland her permanent home.

The only threat to Dorothy's domestic tranquility in Munchkinland is the Wicked Witch of the West. But, as Glinda points out, the Wicked Witch has no power in Munchkinland. In fact, Glinda urges the Witch to leave Munchkinland before someone drops a house on her. The Wicked Witch decides to bide her time and promises Dorothy, "I'll get you, my pretty, and your little dog, too." But Dorothy has nothing to fear. Glinda gives her the ruby slippers, which protect Dorothy from being at the mercy of the Wicked Witch.

The truth is: Dorothy can stay in Munchkinland forever, revered as a national heroine, safeguarded by the ruby slippers, and living under the protective aegis of Glinda, the Good Witch of the North.

Yet, Dorothy, egged on by Glinda, decides to return to Kansas. Why? Munchkinland is a vast improvement over Kansas. Dorothy yearned to fly over the rainbow, but once she gets there, she immediately wants to leave. Isn't that giving up? Isn't leaving Munchkinland surrendering? By wanting to return to Kansas, hasn't Dorothy forsaken her dream?

Of course, Dorothy really doesn't belong in Munchkinland. She's a giant, a fluke, an anomaly, an aberration, a freak show attraction. Living in Munchkinland, Dorothy would be a minority of one, forever out of step with the citizenry. In a sense, Dorothy has to leave Munchkinland for the same reason she had to leave Kansas. In Kansas, Miss Gulch controls half the county and Dorothy is the only person—among the group of inadequate adults on the farm—with the courage to call Miss Gulch a wicked old witch to her face. In Munchkinland, the Wicked Witch of the East controls the Munchkins until Dorothy accidentally frees the little people from tyranny. "Ding Dong! The Witch is dead!" is really a wake-up call for Dorothy to find a new group of friends who share her tenacity and zest for life, friends who are equally unafraid of wicked witches, friends with integrity and verve—like the Scarecrow, the Tin Man, and the Lion.

Dorothy could also make the Emerald City her home. The citizens of the Emerald City welcome her and her three companions with open arms. The Cabby gives them a free carriage ride, led by the Horse of a Different Color, through the glittering streets of the city to the Wash & Brush Up Co., where the Scarecrow is stuffed with fresh straw, the Tin Man is polished, the Lion gets a permanent, and Dorothy is given the opportunity to have her eyes dyed to match her gingham gown. When the Guard to the Palace turns down their request to see the Wizard, Dorothy and her friends can simply call it quits and move into the Emerald City. When they finally get an audience with the Wizard and are told to bring back the broomstick of the Wicked Witch of the West, our heroes could easily refuse to perform this "very small task" and make the Emerald City their home instead.

Then again, there's really no future for Dorothy in the Emerald City. The citizens of the utopian metropolis simply laugh the day away with hedonistic abandon. They proudly admit that they frivolously wake up at noon, start work at one, take an hour for lunch, and finish work by two. It is a narcissistic and self-absorbed society run by a benevolent, faceless dictator. What could Dorothy hope to achieve by making this totalitarian Shangri-la her home?

Dorothy could also live in the castle of the Wicked Witch of the West. Once she kills the Witch (again by accident), the green-faced Winkie Guards and the blue-faced Winged Monkeys drop to their knees and chant, "Hail to Dorothy! The Wicked Witch is dead!" Dorothy and her friends could move into the Witch's Castle and remodel it to their liking, with the Winkies and Winged Monkeys at their beck and call. But living in the Witch's Castle goes completely against Dorothy's nature.

After the Wizard accidentally takes off in his balloon, the Cowardly Lion pleads with Dorothy to stay with them. "But this could never be like Kansas," insists Dorothy, insinuating that there are no dreams for her to dare to dream in the Land of Oz.

Actually, Dorothy gives up her desire to journey over the rainbow before she is swept up by
the cyclone. After consulting with Professor
Marvel and his crystal ball, Dorothy, convinced
she has broken Aunt Em's heart, decides to return
home rather than go along with the Professor to
see all the crowned heads of Europe—even if
it means facing the wrath of Miss Gulch. The
unexpected detour through Oz throws a monkey wrench in her plans, but from the moment
she leaves Professor Marvel, Dorothy never gives
up her desire to return home. Or does she?

There is a distinct difference between your
desire and your intention. If you *desire* to return
home to Kansas, you are attached to the outcome.
You become obsessed with getting back to Kansas.
Intention, on the other hand, is desire without any
attachment to the outcome. You *intend* to return
to Kansas, but you are no longer obsessed with
the idea. Every twist and turn of your journey
through Oz is no longer critical to your ultimate
goal. You no longer feel the need to force solu-
tions. By letting go of your desire and by partic-
ipating with detached involvement, you open

yourself up to infinite possibilities, allowing your destiny to unfold spontaneously—in tune with the fluidity of the cosmos.

Dorothy never seems to give up her attachment to her goal of getting back home to Kansas. Nor does she ever seem to put her life on the line for anyone. In fact, she seems to be nothing more than a self-centered child. Back in Kansas, when Miss Gulch comes to take Toto to the Sheriff and have the dog destroyed, what does Dorothy do? She volunteers to be sent to bed without supper— hardly an act of self-sacrifice. When Toto escapes from Miss Gulch's picnic basket and jumps through the window into Dorothy's room, Dorothy runs away from home to protect Toto from Miss Gulch, never thinking for a moment how this cowardly act will devastate her Aunt Em and Uncle Henry. In the Land of Oz, the Scarecrow, the Tin Man, and the Cowardly Lion all risk their lives for Dorothy. Dorothy, being a child, never risks her life for anyone— until the Wicked Witch orders a Winged Monkey to throw the basket in the river and drown Toto.

Only then does Dorothy risk everything for someone she loves. She willingly lets the Wicked

Witch try to take the ruby slippers from her feet (against Glinda's advice)—even though it means putting herself forever at the Witch's mercy.

Dorothy does indeed surrender. But what she surrenders is her *desire* to get back to Kansas, not her *intention*.

When Dorothy finally detaches herself from the outcome and surrenders to the womb of creation, three incredible things happen. First, Dorothy discovers her profound capacity for self-sacrifice and the extraordinary moral depth of her character. Second, when the Wicked Witch reaches for the ruby slippers, cosmic intervention seems to cause the shoes to suddenly flash like red fire. Third, Toto miraculously escapes, enabling him to bring the Scarecrow, the Tin Man, and the Cowardly Lion back to the Witch's castle to rescue Dorothy.

Detachment allows the intelligence of the universe to help your intentions manifest themselves. When Dorothy is aboard the Wizard's balloon ready to leave for Kansas, Toto does the very thing he did in Kansas that started all of Dorothy's troubles—he chases after a cat. This time, Dorothy chases after Toto, inadvertently letting the Wizard take off in his balloon without her. Dorothy's love for Toto compels her to sacrifice what seems to be her only real chance of returning to Kansas. Had Dorothy been blindly attached to her desire to return home, she might have left Toto behind. After all, bringing Toto back to Kansas will only endanger the dog's life again, since Miss Gulch will inevitably return to have Toto destroyed by the Sheriff (unless a house falls on her too). Toto might be better off staying in the Emerald City. But Dorothy, empowered by the self-knowledge gained from her confrontation with the Wicked Witch of the West, impulsively knows she now has the inner strength to prevent Miss Gulch from destroying Toto. Had Dorothy simply run away with Professor Marvel or returned home again without being swept up by a tornado and sent spiraling to the Land of Oz, she would never possess the courage and self-awareness to save Toto from Miss Gulch's impending return.

The moment Dorothy leaps from the Wizard's hot-air balloon, it is clear that she has given up all attachment to her desire to go home. Only by detaching herself from the outcome—surrendering to the intricate cosmic plan of the universe by sacrificing a return trip home without Toto—does Dorothy earn the karmic right to return home to Kansas.

You too can make the dreams that you dare to dream come true. Like Dorothy, all you need do is surrender your desire to the awesome creative intelligence of the universe.

EIGHT

BRING ME THE
BROOMSTICK OF THE
WICKED WITCH OF
THE WEST

Pᴇᴏᴘʟᴇ ᴜɴᴄᴏɴsᴄɪᴏᴜsʟʏ ᴄᴏᴍᴘᴇᴛᴇ ғᴏʀ ᴇɴᴇʀɢʏ
with each other. You do not need to surrender
your energy to others. You do not need to rob
other people of their energy. The need to give
control to others and the addictive need to
dominate are both obstacles to spiritual enlightenment. The true energy you seek flows abundantly from the creative source of the universe.

When Dorothy, the Scarecrow, the Tin Man,
and the Lion ask for the Wizard's help, the Wizard,

after intimidating and belittling them, says: "The beneficent Oz has every intention of granting your requests! . . . But first you must prove yourselves worthy by performing a very small task." Of course, the task is not small at all. He asks them to risk their lives.

The foursome have no need to prove themselves worthy. They are worthy. By insisting that the four have to prove themselves worthy, the Wizard merely attempts to shatter their self-confidence so he can manipulate them into killing the Wicked Witch of the West. In return, the Wizard promises to grant their requests, attaching strings and conditions to create dependency. The four friends really should question whether the Wizard has the power to grant their requests in the first place, since he obviously doesn't have the power to perform the "very small task" of killing the Wicked Witch himself.

Instead of going after the broomstick of the Wicked Witch of the West, Dorothy could offer the ruby slippers to the Wizard in exchange for a brain, a heart, courage, and a one-way ticket to Kansas. But the thought never crosses her mind (probably because she is clinging to Glinda's warning to never let the ruby slippers off her feet). The Wizard also shows a curious disinterest in the ruby slippers. He definitely knows Dorothy has the mystical shoes. While posing as the Doorman to the Emerald City, the Wizard is alerted by the Scarecrow to the fact that the Good Witch of the North gave Dorothy the ruby slippers. Why then doesn't the Wizard want the sparkling shoes? Does he already have a pair of his own? And, if so, why hasn't he used them against the Wicked Witch of the West?

The Wizard simply may not know that the ruby slippers have any magical powers—proving that he is not as all-knowing as he claims to be. Even if he is aware of their extraordinary power, the Wicked Witch of the West claims to be the only one who knows how to use the ruby slippers—proving yet again that the Wizard is not as all-knowing as he claims to be. If the Wizard does know how powerful the fancy footwear is, why then doesn't he keep the ruby slippers to prevent the witch with the green complexion from getting them? There can only be one explanation: The Wizard fears the Wicked Witch and doesn't want her to come after him for a pair of magical ruby slippers that he doesn't know how to use. Besides, the Wizard's giant disembodied head floating over the throne has no use for shoes anyway. Instead, he bullies Dorothy to use the ruby slippers to do his dirty work.

Dorothy and her friends foolishly allow themselves to be denigrated and controlled by the Wizard. They obsequiously let the Wizard use them as pawns in his struggle to steal energy from the Wicked Witch of the West and control the flow of energy in Oz. By allowing themselves to be manipulated, the foursome fall prey to a typical control drama. Meanwhile, the Witch plans to win all the energy in Oz by robbing Dorothy of her energy (and the ruby slippers) and then using the ruby slippers to control the flow of energy in Oz. The only way Dorothy and her friends can circumvent these pathetic control dramas is by consciously recognizing these destructive energy dynamics. Becoming aware of a power struggle allows you to consciously choose whether to continue it, transform it, or rise above it.

Of course, the Wicked Witch may actually be justified in her crusade. She only wants to get back the ruby slippers, that are rightfully hers—unless her sister stole them from someone else. Her sister's death was an accident, but the embittered Witch of the West, convinced that Dorothy is a threat to her energy, unjustly holds the girl from Kansas accountable. The Witch's distrust and vindictiveness surely justify Glinda's whisking the ruby slippers onto Dorothy's feet to protect the innocent Kansas girl from the green-faced control freak.

Like Miss Gulch, the Wicked Witch is a deeply disturbed individual. She is evil personified. She uses black magic to control others and to acquire more power—all to compensate for her deep-seated neuroses. Inner peace is the harmony between conflicting forces. It is the balance between decency and indecency, between morality and immorality, between spiritual consciousness and base animal needs, between Yin and Yang. When you are wicked, you disrupt this balance. This imbalance then creates a barrier between you and the creative intelligence of the universe. The more you embrace evil, the bigger this chasm becomes, making it easier for your wickedness to continue and condemn you forever— explaining why, as Glinda insists, "Only bad witches are ugly."

To feel in control, the Wicked Witch is obsessed with controlling others—the Winged Monkeys, the Winkie Guards, Dorothy, and ultimately the Emerald City. The Witch, like Miss

Gulch, is a heartless coward, unconsciously convinced that controlling all of Oz and subjugating
all its inhabitants will compensate for her inability to overcome her unresolved subconscious
conflicts. Her obsessive need to control everything
undoubtedly stems from her inability to consciously overcome her lack of self-worth—a deep-
seated neurosis perhaps created by an unresolved
sibling rivalry with her sister, the Wicked Witch of
the East, who had a pair of ruby slippers while
she did not. Like Miss Gulch, the Wicked Witch
does not accept herself the way she is. Instead,
she craves recognition and acquisition as substi-
tutes for love, resulting in a strong need for control. The Witch's main motive is to gain control
over herself—an inward power struggle turned
perversely outward.

Of course, the only way to gain control over
yourself and instill balance and harmony in your
life is to discover your true Self and awaken the
inner spark within you, thus unlocking your own
rich creative potential. Blinded by her obsession
and unable to see the big picture, the Wicked
Witch grasps at straws, relying on black magic to

control others, unlike Glinda, the self-actualized Good Witch, who uses magic to help others gain control over their own destiny. Back in Kansas, Professor Marvel uses a crystal ball to persuade a runaway girl to return home; in Oz, the Wicked Witch of the West uses a crystal ball to prevent Dorothy from returning home. The Wicked Witch savors her own misery. Unfortunately, misery loves company—giving the witch the impetus to use black magic to enslave the Winged Monkeys and the Winkie Guards, robbing them of their energy. Having lost her inner connection with the source of all energy, she resorts to manipulating others so she can steal their energy. (Incidentally, in Zen, monkeys usually symbolize the madness of an unbalanced mind, perhaps explaining why the power-mad Witch is surrounded by them.) The Wicked Witch of the West fails to grasp a basic Zen principle, best expressed by poet Lao-tzu: "For every force there is a counterforce. Violence, even well-intentioned, always rebounds upon itself."

The Wizard of Oz and the Wicked Witch of the West both need to clear away their past programming for controlling the flow of energy. Dorothy and her friends need to clear away their past programming to prevent others from controlling them and to take control of their own lives. The Wizard and the Witch both use intimidation to create an aura of power, when in fact they are most isolated from universal energy. Dorothy, the Scarecrow, the Tin Man, and the Cowardly Lion respond to this control drama by being meek and small to elicit sympathy to regain the flow of energy.

You can break free from your pattern of control and survival. By discovering your true Self, by tapping into the universal source of all energy, by becoming aware of your control dramas, you can transform your control dramas into attributes. Instead of trying to elicit sympathy, you will use your compassion to help others, just like the Scarecrow, Tin Man, and Cowardly Lion use their compassion to help Dorothy and then to rule the Emerald City once the Wizard leaves. Instead of trying to intimidate others like the Wizard, you will drop your illusion of power and use your leadership skills to help others get in touch with their true power.

On the other hand, if you, like the Wicked Witch of the West, refuse to give up your control drama, convinced that you can control everything, you will eventually self-destruct. Good always prevails over evil because evil ultimately dissolves itself.

Back in Kansas, Zeke (the Cowardly Lion's alter ego) urges Dorothy to have a little courage and spit in Miss Gulch's eye. In a way, Dorothy does spit in her eye. She throws a bucket of water at the Scarecrow's flaming arm, splashing the Wicked Witch in the eyes. As the Wicked Witch melts, she curses Dorothy. "Who would have thought a good little girl like you could destroy my beautiful wickedness?" she asks. As it is written in the *Tao Te Ching:*

Nothing in the world
Is as soft and yielding as water.
Yet, for dissolving the hard
      and inflexible,
Nothing can surpass it.

カーテンの後にいるヤツなんか気にするな

NINE

PAY NO ATTENTION TO THAT MAN BEHIND THE CURTAIN

PEOPLE CAN CHANGE YOUR LIFE FOR THE better. They can inspire you, challenge you, motivate you, and help you recognize who you really are. Inspiring people are gentle souls full of light and joy. Uninspiring people abuse power. They pretend to help you when all they are really doing is manipulating you to help themselves. You must learn to tell the difference between a person who is truly influential and full of light and a humbug hiding behind a curtain.

Glinda, the Good Witch of the North, suggests that the only person who may know how Dorothy might get back to Kansas would be "the great and wonderful Wizard of Oz himself." She describes the Wizard as "very good, but very mysterious." Dorothy has no idea who the Wizard is, what his credentials might be, or what makes him worthy of her admiration. Yet, she holds the Wizard in high regard based solely on Glinda's oblique endorsement. The song Dorothy sings as she skips down the Yellow Brick Road attempts to explain why she considers the Wizard her savior, but fails to offer any logical justification for her confidence in the Wizard's ability to provide help:

> *We're off to see the Wizard,*
> *The Wonderful Wizard of Oz.*
> *We hear he is a whiz of a Wiz,*
> *If ever a Wiz there was.*
> *If ever, oh ever a Wiz there was,*
> *The Wizard of Oz*
> *Is one because . . .*
> *Because, because, because, because,*
> *   because. . . .*

Because of the wonderful things he
   does.
We're off to see the Wizard,
The Wonderful Wizard of Oz.

The Wizard is purported to be a whiz of a Wiz because—and note how many times Dorothy repeats the word *because* to give herself more time to think up a suitable explanation—of the wonderful things he does. Neither Glinda nor the Munchkins list even one wonderful thing the Wizard has specifically accomplished. All we know for certain is that the Wizard has failed to rid Oz of either the Wicked Witch of the East or the Wicked Witch of the West, proving that his powers are severely limited. Yet Dorothy, convinced that the mysterious Wizard is her only hope for returning to Kansas, persuades the Scarecrow, the Tin Man, and the Cowardly Lion to accompany her to ask the Wizard for a brain, a heart, and courage. She leads a pilgrimage to find an enigmatic Wizard she has never met, blindly revering him as a kind of maharishi, guru, buddha, shaman, sorcerer, or swami—never questioning whether the Wizard she seeks might be a false prophet.

When Toto reveals the timid little man behind the curtain, the Wizard offers a feeble explanation. "I'm an old Kansas man myself. . . . Born and bred in the heart of the western wilderness, premier balloonist par excellence to the Miracle Wonderland Carnival Company—until one day, while performing spectacular feats of stratospheric skill never before attempted by civilized man, an unfortunate phenomena occurred. The balloon failed to return to the fair."

The Wizard explains that the winds brought the balloon down into the heart of the Emerald City, where its citizens proclaimed him "Oz, the First Wizard deluxe." Being an opportunist, he promptly seized power ("retaining my balloon against the advent of a quick getaway," he admits)—in contrast to Dorothy, who, after falling from the sky into Munchkinland, honorably refuses to accept the title of good witch or bad witch. We never learn anything about the Emerald City's previous leader or whether the Wizard's predecessor was peace-

fully deposed, ruthlessly exiled, or mercilessly
executed.

We do know that as the ruler of the Emerald
City, the Wizard is inaccessible to his loyal sub-
jects, sequestering himself in a throne room with
a complex device that projects him as a gigantic
green head floating over a throne between two
urns spewing flames and smoke. To prevent the
citizens of Oz from seeing through his smoke
and mirrors, the paranoid Wizard poses as the
Doorman to the Emerald City, the Cabby with
the Horse of a Different Color, and the Guard
to the Palace to screen his callers and prevent
anyone from having an audience with him. As
long as the Wizard remains unreachable and
mysterious, the people cannot unmask him as an
imposter.

When our weary heroes arrive at the front
gate and ask to see the Wizard, the Wizard, masquerading as the Doorman, responds, "Nobody
can see the Great Oz! Nobody's ever seen the
Great Oz! Even *I've* never seen him!" The Wizard inadvertently reveals that the all-knowing,
all-powerful Wizard of Oz is a myth that he has

allowed the gullible citizenry of the Emerald City to perpetuate. Yet Dorothy never questions why a wizard with a wonderful reputation makes himself inaccessible to his people.

On one level, *The Wizard of Oz* is a warning against blindly following leaders or expecting them to solve your problems. The Wizard, while claiming to be "beneficent," rules Oz through fear and intimidation—from behind a curtain. He extols himself as "the Great and Powerful Oz" while insulting the Tin Man and the Scarecrow, frightening the Cowardly Lion, and silencing an infuriated Dorothy by calling her a "whippersnapper."

But there is something deeper going on here. Why would the citizens of the Emerald City make this fraudulent man their leader simply because he fell from the skies in a hot-air balloon? Maybe the citizens of Oz were so desperate to defend themselves against the Wicked Witch of the West that they eagerly anointed the befuddled stranger who miraculously floated down from the heavens as their leader in the hopes that he would give them the protection they needed. Wouldn't it then make sense for the impotent Wizard to sequester himself in the Throne Room and devise an elaborate illusion to keep the Wicked Witch of the West at bay?

Intimidated by the illusion of the Great and Powerful Oz, the Wicked Witch is afraid to materialize in a cloud of red smoke in the Emerald City like she does in Munchkinland. Instead she flies over the city at a safe distance on her broom and writes a pathetic "Surrender Dorothy" in the sky in black smoke.

When the Wizard discovers that Dorothy is "the Witch's Dorothy," he orders her to "Go Away!" and leave the Emerald City in peace. Then he realizes that Dorothy, having killed the Wicked Witch of the East, might be the answer to his problem. He intimidates Dorothy and her friends with his laser light show, then tells them he has every intention of granting their requests if—and only if—they "bring me the broomstick of the Wicked Witch of the West."

If Dorothy and her friends somehow succeed, the Emerald City will be free from the threat of the Wicked Witch of the West once and for all, and the Wizard will be liberated from his self-imposed seclusion. If, as in all likelihood, the Witch kills Dorothy and her friends first, the Wizard's reputation will remain untarnished, and he will be rid of the troublesome Kansas farm girl whose mere presence in the Emerald City provokes the Witch's wrath. Either way, the Wizard wins—unless, of course, the Wicked Witch gets the ruby slippers and they actually give her the additional power she needs to take over the Emerald City (proving that the Wizard is hardly a whiz of a Wiz).

When you put your trust in someone who lacks integrity and compassion to solve your problems, chances are that someone will use you as a pawn to solve their own problems. If you find yourself going after the broomstick of the Wicked Witch of the West because an intimidating large green head floating over a throne and spewing fire promised to grant your request for help if you prove yourself worthy, maybe you should ask yourself, "Why am I allowing someone else to control my life?" As the *Tao Te Ching* says: "If you look to others for fulfillment, you will never truly be fulfilled."

When Dorothy and her friends return with the broomstick, the Wizard is astonished to see them, never having expected them to survive—let alone having to make good on his promise to grant their requests. Caught off guard, he stalls, insisting they come back tomorrow. But Dorothy, having confronted the Wicked Witch, is no longer "Dorothy, the Meek and Small." When she demands that the Wizard keep his promise, he rages, "Do not arouse the wrath of the Great and Powerful Oz!" But Dorothy refuses to be intimidated anymore. "If you were really great and powerful," she admonishes, "you'd keep your promises!"

When Toto pulls the curtain aside, revealing the Wizard speaking into a microphone, throwing levers, and spinning control knobs, the Wizard shouts the words echoed by dictators throughout history: "Pay no attention to that man behind the curtain!"

The Scarecrow, Tin Man, and Cowardly Lion correctly identify the Wizard as "a humbug."

"You're a very bad man," chastises Dorothy.

"Oh, no, my dear," offers the Wizard. "I'm a very good man. I'm just a very bad Wizard."

But is the Wizard really a good man? If the Wizard were truly great and powerful, he never would send Dorothy and her friends on a suicide mission in the first place. True, he forces Dorothy to confront her worst fears, the same way Professor Marvel sends Dorothy back home to Aunt Em, where she will inevitably be forced to confront Miss Gulch. And yes, the Wizard, by forcing Dorothy to confront an inadequate adult, does become the catalyst for her spiritual growth, through which she learns to take control of her own destiny. But that's all accidental. The Wizard's only intention is to remain in power by protecting the citizens of the Emerald City from the Wicked Witch of the West. To do that, he's willing to sacrifice the lives of Dorothy and her friends. That's not exactly a testimony to the wonderful things he supposedly does.

Dorothy makes the Wizard face up to the fact that he has protected the people of the Emerald City with very little brains, heart, or courage. Humiliated, the Wizard tries to make amends. He gives the Scarecrow, the Tin Man, and the Cowardly Lion awards—a diploma, a testimonial, and a medal—in recognition of the qualities they had all along, and then volunteers to take Dorothy back to the land of *E Pluribus Unum*.

But what the Wizard really gives the Scarecrow, Tin Man, and Cowardly Lion is a valuable spiritual lesson, namely that you already possess the attributes you seek most passionately, regardless if those traits receive recognition from outside authorities. The Scarecrow, Tin Man, and Cowardly Lion fail to heed the message and grab their trophies.

Before leaving the Emerald City to hobnob with his fellow wizards, the Wizard appoints the Scarecrow to be his successor "by virtue of his highly superior brains," even though he has never witnessed any display of the Scarecrow's intelligence. By failing to choose a successor from among the citizens of the Emerald City, the Wizard reveals how out of touch he is with his own people. He could call for free elections, but instead flaunts his total disregard for democracy, proving once and for all that he is indeed "a very bad wizard."

If you put all your faith in someone else to solve your problems, it is because you are lacking faith in yourself. When you have little respect for yourself, you can be easily manipulated by people who see this vulnerability in you— because you do not see it in yourself. To become self-reliant, you must trust your own inner nature and love yourself. Then, if the Wizard tells you to bring back the broomstick of the Wicked Witch of the West, you will pay absolutely no attention to that man behind the curtain.

TEN

THERE'S NO PLACE
LIKE HOME

> *When they think that they know the*
> *answers,*
> *People are difficult to guide.*
> *When they know that they don't,*
> *People can find their own way.*
> —*Tao Te Ching*

THE PATH TO ENLIGHTENMENT IS A PERSONAL
journey. No one can hand you the answer on a
silver platter. "The basic position of Zen is that
it has nothing to say, nothing to teach," wrote

Alan Watts in *The Way of Zen*. "The truth of Buddhism is so self-evident, so obvious that it is, if anything, concealed by explaining it. Therefore the master does not 'help' the student in any way, since helping would actually be hindering."

Dorothy puts all her faith and trust in the Wizard to get her back home, even after Toto reveals him to be a fraud. The Wizard promises to take her back to Kansas in his balloon, but only after the balloon accidentally takes off without Dorothy does the Wizard reveal that he doesn't know how to work it. Glinda, the Good Witch of the North, on the other hand, is a true Zen Master. She doesn't tell Dorothy the answers. Instead, she sets Dorothy on a path toward self-enlightenment.

When Dorothy learns to stop allowing other people to control her life, when she stops putting her faith in others to solve her problems, when she discovers her inner spark, she attains satori, the Zen experience of awakening. When Glinda tells her, "You've always had the power to go back to Kansas," Dorothy "awakens" to the realization that her heart's desire is an inward journey, not an outward one; and though her true

Self may not be apparent, it still resides deep within.

Glinda explains that she did not share this truth with Dorothy earlier because Dorothy had to learn it for herself.

Instead, Glinda tells Dorothy upon arriving in Munchkinland, "The sooner you get out of Oz altogether, the safer you'll sleep my dear"— despite the fact that Dorothy is welcome to stay in Munchkinland (where the Wicked Witch of the West has no power) protected by the ruby slippers on her feet. When Dorothy asks how she can possibly return to Kansas, Glinda insists, "The only person who might know would be the great and wonderful Wizard of Oz himself."

But this isn't true at all. The Wizard isn't the only person who knows how Dorothy can get back to Kansas. Glinda knows. Why is she lying? And why do the Munchkins bow reverently at the mere mention of a Wizard who was obviously unable to free them from the tyranny of the Witch of the East? It's possible that Glinda is simply being obtuse. She specifically describes the Wizard as "the only person who might know" how Dorothy can get back home to Kansas. The Wizard *might* know, unlike Glinda, who *definitely* knows. Also, unlike the Wizard, Glinda is not technically a person; she is a witch with supernatural powers, thus making the Wizard the only *person* who *might* know.

But that's all petty semantics. Glinda is still telling Dorothy a half-truth. Why does Glinda, a self-proclaimed good witch, intentionally mislead Dorothy and send her on a perilous journey fraught with danger? Doesn't that make her a bad witch?

Strange as it may seem, a Zen Master's role is to intentionally mislead the student by putting obstacles and barriers in the student's path. "This is like encouraging the growth of a hedge by pruning," explains Alan Watts in *The Way of Zen*, "for obviously, the basic intention is to help, but the Zen student does not really know Zen unless he finds it out for himself." Knowledge cannot be taught, it must be gained from experience. As the Zen poet Jeremy Wolff so eloquently wrote: "Experience isn't the best teacher, it's the only teacher."

Like the Zen Master impeding a student from solving a koan (Zen riddle), Glinda cleverly obstructs Dorothy by sending her down the Yellow Brick Road to seek outside help from the wonderful Wizard of Oz. In reality, Dorothy should look in the opposite direction. Dorothy will find the way home—the way back to her true essence—within herself, not from outside sources. Glinda knows full well that the Wizard is a fraud who will manipulate Dorothy into killing the Wicked Witch of the West for him. But she also knows that Dorothy is perfectly safe as long as she wears the ruby slippers. And when the Wicked Witch puts a poisonous field of deadly poppies in Dorothy's path, Glinda makes it snow, counteracting the poppies' poisonous scent and revealing that she has the power to help Dorothy at any time.

When Glinda abruptly leaves, floating away in a pink bubble, the flabbergasted Kansas girl remarks, "My! People come and go so quickly here!" Dorothy makes a startling discovery. Time is fleeting. Eternity is now, the moment of the present. As an ancient Zen poet wrote, "Do not dwell in the past, do not dream of the future, concentrate the mind on the present moment." The way to live in the present is to remember that "This too shall pass." When you experience joy, remembering that "This too shall pass" helps you savor the here and now. When you experience pain or sorrow, remembering that "This too shall pass" reminds you that grief, like joy, is only temporary. To appreciate your loved ones, to count your blessings, or to simply stop and smell the roses, tell yourself "This too shall pass" and you will instantly be here now.

When the Scarecrow and the Tin Man insist upon making sure Dorothy gets safely to the Wizard, Dorothy exclaims, "Oh, you're the best friends anybody ever had! And it's funny, but I feel as if I've known you all the time—but I couldn't have, could I?"

"I don't see how," deduces the Scarecrow. "You weren't around when I was stuffed and sewn together, were you?"

"And I was standing over there, rusting for the longest time," laments the Tin Man.

"Still—I wish I could remember," insists Dorothy. "But I guess it doesn't matter, anyway. We know each other now, don't we?"

In a flash, Dorothy decides to be here now.

When you embrace the present, when you immerse yourself in the here and now, when you become one with the moment, you experience the pure joy of the cosmos. You unite with the ecstacy sparkling throughout the universe. You experience each moment as an exultant expression of creation, filled with pure potential and abundant love. As the *Tao Te Ching* says:

> *Be content with what you have;*
> *Rejoice in the way things are.*
> *When you realize there is nothing*
>   *lacking,*
> *The whole world belongs to you.*

Now is the moment of all creation. Now is the moment of all potential. Now is the moment of infinite possibilities. Now is an eternal gift. Coming to this realization is liberating.

It has been said that if you want to change the world, you must first change yourself. Living a life of love and service begins with the desire to center your life on the source of correct morals, ethics, and principles. That source is your intrinsic essence, your true Self, the inner spark within you.

French philosopher Pierre Teilhard de Chardin said it best: "We are not human beings having a spiritual experience. We are spiritual beings having a human experience."

When you discover the true essence of your inner spark, when you embrace your spiritual nature, when you live in the here and now, when you are at home with yourself, the creative energy of the cosmic intelligence will flow abundantly and harmoniously, propelling you to fulfill your cosmic purpose easily and effortlessly.

Then you will truly know with all your heart, with all your might, and with all your soul:

There's no place like home.

ACKNOWLEDGMENTS

I deeply love my wife Debbie for her highly superior brain, her magnificent heart, and her outstanding courage. Her invaluable insights, wisdom, warmth, deep spirituality, and unconditional love inspired this book.

My daughter Ashley listened with awe and wonder as I read from L. Frank Baum's *Oz* books before putting her to bed each night, and together we watched *The Wizard of Oz* almost as many times as her younger sister Julia has seen *Toy Story*.

May the dreams that they dare to dream always come true.

I am grateful to my editor, Richard F. X. O'Connor, for encouraging me to follow the Yellow Brick Road, to my agent, Jeremy Solomon, for helping me get to the Emerald City, to my copy editor, Elizabeth von Radics, for representing the Lullaby League, to Patric Verrone for representing the Lollipop Guild, to artist extraordinaire Cathy Pavia, for being the Good Witch of the North, to my sister, Amy Sue, and my brothers, Douglas and Michael, for being my Scarecrow, Tin Man, and Lion, and to my parents, Bob and Barbara Green, for always encouraging me to reveal the man behind the curtain and for making sure I always know there's no place like home.

At Warner Bros., I am indebted to Judy Singer, Judy Noack, Paula Allen, Roger Mayer, and Rosemary Gawelko for granting the necessary permissions to help me escape from the clutches of the Wicked Witch of the West. I am also grateful to the Great and Powerful Bill Hartley at Renaissance Books for helping me

click my ruby slippers together to get back
home to Kansas.

Joey Green is a best-selling author with a gift for blending the timeless wisdom of Eastern spirituality with rich and enduring icons of American pop culture. He is also executive director of the Oz Institute in Woodland Hills, California, and publishes a quarterly newsletter called *The Oz Principle.*